WRITING LETTERS TO MORRISON

JACQUELINE MILOM

Outskirts Press, Inc.
Denver, Colorado

Writing Letters to Morrison
All Rights Reserved.
Copyright © 2008 Jacqueline Milom
V2.0

Outskirts Press, Inc.
http://www.outskirtspress.com

ISBN: 978-1-4327-1776-6

Outskirts Press and the "OP" logo are trademarks belonging to Outskirts Press, Inc.

PRINTED IN THE UNITED STATES OF AMERICA

For My Panda Bear

ACKNOWLEDGMENTS

If you look deep inside yourself, you find there are many inspirations. Life, love, breathing, dreaming and just simply an Idol. My poetic "Idol" I have never met, will never meet, and is no longer with us. He had a way with words though. This Idol is Jim Morrison. I've listened to my father's Doors records and always been fascinated by Jim. One day my older sister Melissa gave me a poetry book of Jim's. A collection of his works. I read it almost everyday. I took it to school with me and when I had the chance I'd read it again and again. I would rather sit there and read that book than listen to my chemistry teacher. I had actually sat there and read the book under the desk. She often didn't pay attention to whether or not I was paying attention. I failed chemistry. Figures I never understood Chemistry anyways. I had lost that book. Missy bought me a new one for my 24th Birthday. It was both times, one of my favorite gifts ever. Thank you Missy for giving me that book. I love you with all my heart.

This poetic book Writing Letters to Morrison is dedicated to Jim. Wherever he may be. It is also dedicated to my other "Idol" Mr. White. Mr. White was my creative writing teacher. He was my favorite teacher in the whole wide world. He often made me smile in class. He made me enjoy coming to school and I hated school with a passion. I was and still am at times, a shy little one. I hated presentations. I'd feel sick and nervous if I had to get up in front of the class and speak. Mr. White would always say "Jackie one day you and I are going to tap dance in front of the class". He made me laugh every time. We never tap danced. He is no longer a teacher at my high school. His class was the only class I wouldn't sneak Jim under the desk. Mr. White I miss and adore you. Thanks so much.

Kacie Kugel. Beautiful created lies. Great friend and inspiration. Thank you for reading my unfinished works, and for listening to me talk of Jim Morrison, poets and the world of writing. If I ever get into trouble before a rock concert you'll be the first one I call.

Tisha a fellow poet. I read your works and they sound too much like mine. I mean that in the best sense. We are both on the same path with our writings and I wish you great success with yours. I dedicate this to you and poets in this lovely world. I think life is nothing without a little bit of poetry even if it's not written down. I think everyone can find "poetry" in anything.

I'd also love to say thank you to Matt Wachter. I am happy to share my poems with you as long as you enjoy them. Your endless positive feedback is what makes me want to share more. It could've been anyone. Just that great feedback. Honestly, you've had a bigger reaction to anything I've written than most people I've encountered. That means a lot to me. I appreciate it.

MY ANGELS

breathing in the silence
watching with a curious eye
something burning inside and dying quickly
a sincere perplexity and it is carrying me away
consumed by a nonchalant state
I dive right into it
feeding off the blood of it
my heaven has gone
and my angels too
but maybe I'll look up
and find them
til then I'll sit in lonliness
a dark comforting fear
my heaven has gone
and my angels too
but maybe I'll look up
and find them
til then I sit in lonliness

SOME PLACE COLD

I wandered someplace cold today
I felt that maybe you would come out of hiding
That maybe you'd look in the mirror and stop judging
and that maybe you'd have something powerful to say
Confidence is just an image
Self love is something real
Dwelling is a feeling
Consumption is a danger
I wandered someplace cold today
Did you come out of hiding?
Did you look in the mirror and stop judging
Did you have something powerful to say
I suppose you did
Confidence is definitely an image as
Self love is beyond real.

SHOOT DOWN

bitter mind. breathe and shoot down
writings on the ceiling
parting ways
Don't remember me
Tell me to see
to be free
but you trap me
trap me inside
this torn mind
go away now.
jump into a hole
walking slowly
feeding into me
back to the wrong path
Where is it going to go?
Nowhere to nowhere
A savior in the past
bitter mind. breathe and shoot down.

MENTAL SELF MUTILATION

The depressed feeling
that feeds into my vein
lingering here without end
shove it down and away
I'll lay down in this
and try to feel beyond it
seeping tears that won't defend
hurt everyone just to hurt yourself
blackened heart killed me
this mental self mutilation
it bleeds, takes, gives, and takes more
the aching control
that tells you that
you've lost it all
There is nothing to make it stop
but to become numb until
a new feeling arises
Then it'll feed into my vein
lingering here without end
shove it down and away

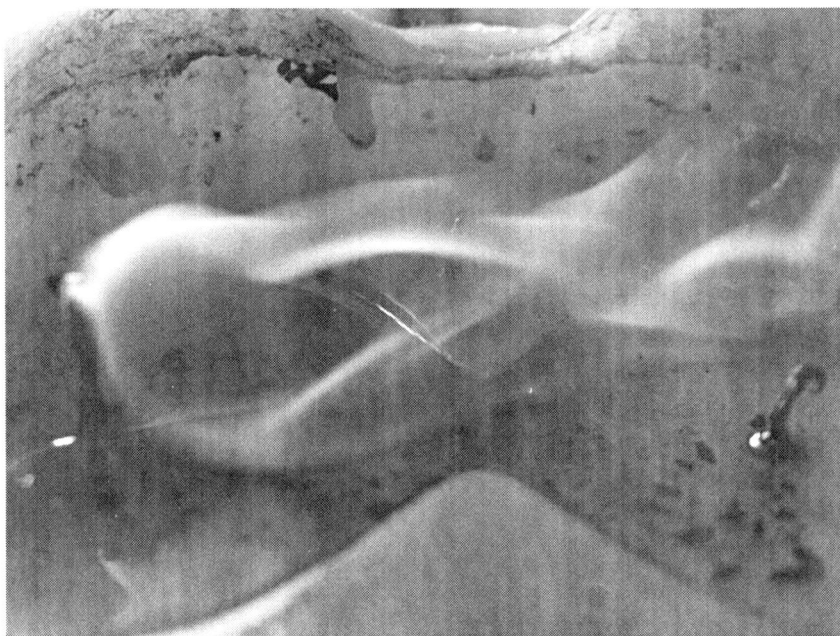

A RANDOM MEANINGLESS ACT

To find nothing important is a tradegy
Life is more than a random meaningless act
You are heartless and confining
You are brainless and numb
and you give lies to justify what you lack
Curious we are when we are too lazy to find the answers
Wondering is what we do when we can't find the answers
You are careless and controlling
You are belligerent and dumb
Yes to find nothing important is a tradegy
and life has to be more than a random meaningless act

LEGAL DRUG

Happy to be alone
Happy to smile and feel free
dancing to Rome
grow up and move on
No one can hold you down
without your consent
Spinnning, and feeling high
imagination is my drug
living is my drug
love is my drug
Don't piss me off
I won't listen anymore
I don't dare to dream
of bitter infatuation when I am gone
and all is sore
Needing no one but
the one
is perfect and til
I find who I need
I don't need you
to make me feel
like this fool
I'm a dreamer
and I once read
Don't let your dreams be dreams
No one can hold you down
without your consent

FREE SPIRIT

A free spirit
drifting from nowhere
what shall I see?
Who shall I be?
Lovely gain and all
that fills dreams!
a creation from happiness
mysterious and gorgeous
broken no more
shouting yes
no negativity left
you told me very little
but it makes sense
to be this content
my lovely gain and all
that fills my dreams
A free spirit

CHANGING SHADES

changing to a different shade
making sure not to waste the important
and when it all goes away
I will hold on to it for another day
wishing for the sun
needing for a time
crashing all around me
and not knowing what is mine
if only I could see
if only I could be
changing to a different shade
and when it all goes away
I will hold on to it for another day

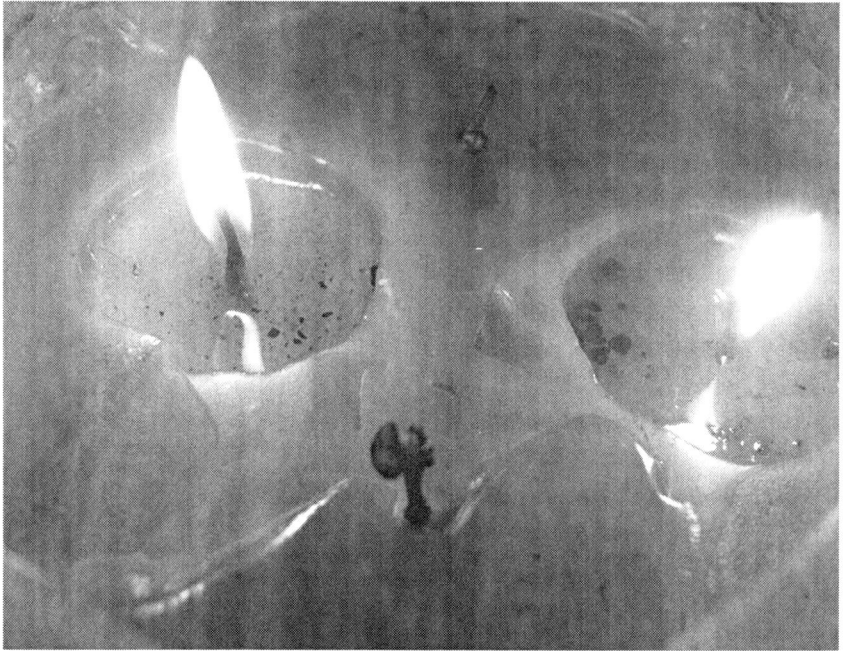

ONCE BEFORE

The things we hide
one day I'll have strength
with love on my side
I saw it once before
and if I knew it would be no more
I would've held on
held on so tight
with all my might
all the greatness I can't find
but one day I'll have strength
with love on my side
I have seen it once before
and If I knew it could be no more
I would've held on so tight
I would've put up a fight
Oh the things we hide

THOUGHTFUL DEMISE

beautifully defined
clearly falling and lost
sharpened heart
with such a thoughtful demise
she watched the missed
heart breaking yet still together
that one torn feeling
caught between love, like
and despise.
unsure and unclear
where was myself
when he decided
to bring a hurt thick
it's a call to a desperate
when we all know
heartbreak is fickle
yes a thoughtful demise

MY LIFE

Belittled and changing
it is such a strange world
I keep growing farther from reality
maybe one day I can see clearly
and maybe one day you can hear me
when is it we stop searching
and start living
when is it we stop judging
and start giving
People hide behind it all
I guess I should stop being a person
when my dreams break my fall
People run from the cold
I guess I should start being a person
before I grow old
I only have so little time
in a world filled with curiosities
I only have one life
in a world filled with falsified imagery
I guess I should start living and breathing

SOULS

Souls are the inner self we all want
Souls are the inner belief skeptics taunt
Meaning is something the world needs
but few are willing to give it
The hope just sits there and bleeds
Are you fearless or lifeless?
To you what is the difference?
Knowing more than I desire
and it is nothing new
Souls are the life we all fight for
Souls are the fight we all live for
Deepness is something we all should find
Pettiness is something we all should hide
Souls are the inner self I want
Souls are the inner belief that I taunt
Meaning is something the world needs
and if you aren't willing to give it then I am

A JADED PLACE

A jaded place to go
blackness piercing through me
harder than anything
sinking in and breaking me
Bleeding, cutting, and carelessness
secrets coming out of hiding
something fierce and finding
looking at an old playground
through a dark way
shallowness engulfs us
then I have to go deeper
just to feel something
whispers in the lonely places
that we ignore
shut out the screams
right?

A DEEPENED HEART

A deepened heart
slowly draining and dying
a shallow look
selfish? who can't be
drowning in these words
these words you can never see
Crash into me
Burn me. choke me. shake me.
You don't know these eyes
but you pretend very well
pretend. slash. bite.
hate me no more than
you love me.
lay low and feel strong
one day you'll learn
A deepened heart
slowly draining and dying.

CLOSE THE EYES

close the eyes
runaway but come back
gripping someone
a fight of sadness
you lost all my hope
break my darkness
without the fear of humans
can you look into me
and tell me why I shouldn't hate?
shouldn't hate as you hate
praying and wanting
yet someone is bleeding
I crumbled to pieces
as well as my heart today
close my eyes

A PERFECT CALM

This perfect calm.
Waters rising away
fears drifting
the storm has gone
I am free of damage
my own life
I am better now
misery gone
nothing but being free
free of it all
lifting higher
til it is my own face
my own place
just finding a path
that is no longer sad
letting go of distrust
and hatred
finally I am breathing
breathing so hard
bury bad
consume by good
the perfect calm.

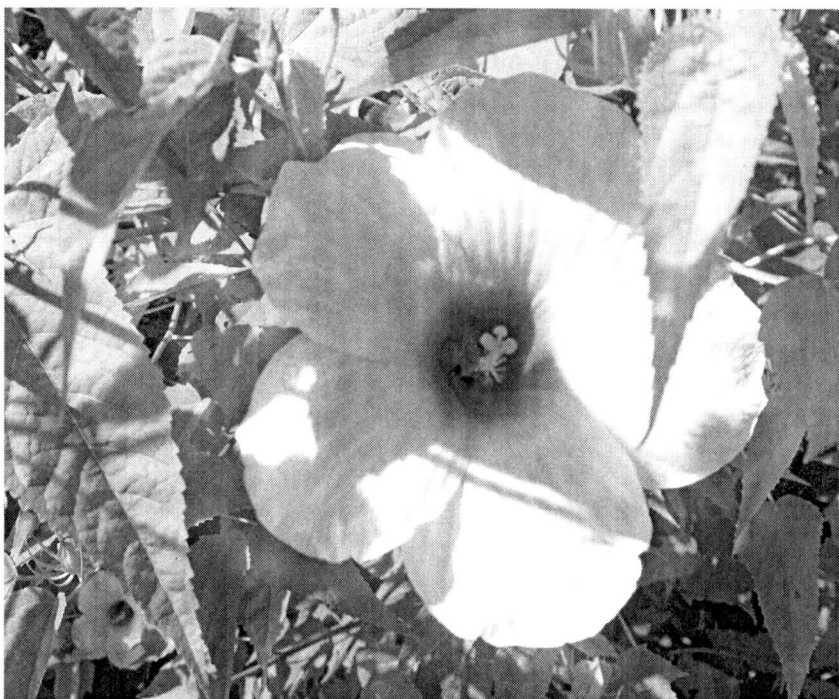

DADDY

sitting with too many thoughts
If I could stop them all
and not think about what if
it made me cry today
and all has been said,
that I have to say
I feel like you don't care
and I can't take it
I was a little girl
who wanted to know her daddy
now I am a little girl that does,
or at least more.
I don't want to let go
but today the possiblity hit
will you listen to me?
If I just talked?
my sisters talked.
It starts to seem that, I
know nothing anymore
I can't take it
ten years?
that will fly by quick
you told baby sister,
you told her well you always have him
well that isn't the same
he is like a you to me,
but the second is never like the original

you are the one and only dad
and I want you to stop talking the way
the way you seem to talk.
one day on the way home
a converstation made it clear
we were a lot alike and I hold that dear

COURAGE

tired and shaking
a world unknown
A blindness here for the taking
fiercely jaded
with a heart so faded
I need a grip
a real strong grip
I suppose courage is in the eye
the eye of the beholder
where is my safety
where is my savior
I suppose courage is something you
something you learn
can I get back up
Can I get back up
Now that I'm so far down
Where is my safety?
Where is my savior?
I suppose courage is something I
something I need to see
I need a grip
a real strong grip
Oh the courage

THE GIRL AND THE WOMAN

The shy little girl stood still
and yet she wandered
Thinking will I go far?
Quiet and hidden
feeling great was too hard
The bold little woman stood tall
and yet she felt small
Could I go far?
Quiet and no longer hidden
Maybe feeling great isn't so hard
Dreams come and dreams go, but little girls
and little women have everything to show

LOOKING THROUGH MYSELF

looking harder through myself
I'm learning and breathing more
seeing everything anew
and bending for no one
no man, no woman
no infatuation, no lust, no friend
picking up my heart's pieces
fixing my trust
and mending my flaws
I have a happier outlook
that you won't break anymore
nothing even for a score
nothing holding me back
nothing to care too much about
no respect to give out
to be the better person
just respect
for myself and you
you can't look through me
you'll never figure me
I'm learning and breathing more

BEAUTIFULLY NEW

completely finding
wondering in a mist of you
an oblivious search
coming into life and
comforting silence
waiting and pretty
beautifully new
shot away from life
and beautifully new

NORMALCY

Some sort of normalcy
divine right?
perhaps? but where is the line
do we draw it faster and clearer?
or do we hide from it all?
Something funny lurks
and it provokes
breathes us into nothing
feeding on lost hope
mindless or mindful?
Can it be both?
let's divide and conquer
our places
breathe to succeed
wanting more and all
without one single fall
it's impossible
but we'll get back up again
and live some sort of normalcy

BLEED INTO ME

The love of darkness
bleeds into me
no more thoughts today
Leave me for peace
I knew your hurt
and It doesn't belong in me
cold hands, and tears of bitterness
It's your fault
down to every drop of hate
down to every drop of letting go
without a single dime of forgiveness
a single thought for myself
is my release
This love of darkness
it bleeds into me.

ADDICTION TO INFATUATION

some sort of frivolous insanity
Let's go live on the moon
Let's go fly high
just be far away
Such a content to fall
madly in like
the world is yours in everyone eyes
distinctly in happiness
it won't last long
so hold on
falling hard is the easy part
coming away from it all
will leave you with nothing
but you'll be fine
after the fall
of falling very hard
It is what infatuations are made of
Someday the addiction to them will fade
Someday you will be content to be alone
Someday you will just be content
to only know yourself
It is all frivolous insanity

CRY FOR

can you find me
breathe me?
seek me?
it's there and haunting
I cry for it
I scream for it
and you bite
losing dreams fast
calm and the old
grey cold skies
as we meet for
the final time
drained of all my love
as were too far gone
will you find me?

PERFECT ON MY OWN

Different words
yet all the same actions
You take back it all
and cause your fall
where in all this did I matter?
you tell me a friendship
but what you want is
just a little bit of everything
I'm not a convenience
one can't want another
whenever they feel they should
your words start to shatter,
and I don't give a shit anymore
I am letting all associations go
I need less of you
and you never needed me
all my words you would never see
So leave me alone
I'm perfect on my own

IF LIES WERE REAL

If lies were real
life could make sense
it's dark and changing
in such a sincere way
An empty face to stay
pleading for nothing
gain me or not
look through my eyes
find me complete
Breathe through a world
so disgusting and vile
It's the interpretation of the lost
If lies were real
We'd might feel real

HURTFUL FRIEND

To find something right
is to be utterly wrong
am I normal yet?
What is normal?
upsetting at the least
his eyes say everything
not love, but a terrible like
that leads into dislike
why do I let it get to me
when I can't really see
where the beauty is
in having someone at all
perhaps another sucks
the beauty right out
and leaves me with nothing
but hate
and wondering about what
I have.
What do I have?
a friend that hurts

TRAGIC OPINION

With such a lost beauty
I laid desperately
and a waterfall coming down
my torn face
what a tragic opinion of myself
oh I'm scattered all over the place
do you know I like to break mirrors
do you know I like to put me down
with such a lost beauty
I lay desperately
and a waterfall coming down
my torn face
A tragic opinion of myself
do I love thee
do I like thee
NO! NO! NO! NO!
If only I could see
do you know I like to break mirrors
do you know I like to put me down
Such a tragic opinion of myself

LOST GIRL

A lost little girl
looking through her glass
pondering places
perplexed and complicated
faithfully stuck
Her tears are hard on her
her love burns
oh how she hates the world
lost little girl
pondering places
forgetting faces
hating the world
hating the world
She wants to run away
Fly away
Jump away
Anything at all
I am she
and she is me

FINDING NEW

Finding something new or
just fading out?
No one seems to know
feeling fine and feeling free
Now what will ensue?
No one will ever know
You are stuck and you are lost
Sorry can't help you
You have no answers
and I won't have a question
Finding something new or just fading out?
I believe you answered that

OLD WISDOM

old wisdom
bitter dreams
fighting hard
and making nothing
beautiful ending
Graceful emptiness passing
oh how beautiful
the sight of broke love
hide around me
find me here
freedom is a choice
we don't take

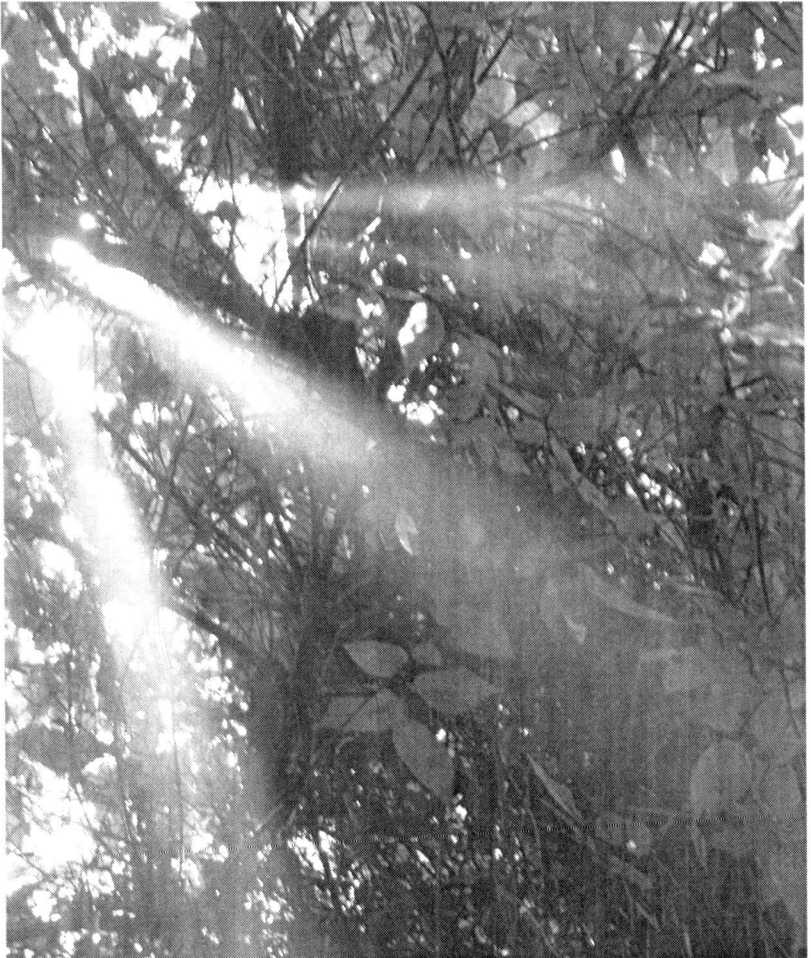

FIX ME

If I could fix this
mend it so tight
get what he wants
and still maintain me
where does this go
anywhere at all?
it bleeds so
hate and like
spiraling from me.
where are my wishes?
are they cared for?
stop this and leave me be
I can't talk right now
I can't think right now
my mind is sore
and tired of you and I

AFRAID TO BE ALONE

Shallow deep
someday I'll go somewhere
amongst the light
drained from heartfelt sadness
coming closer to shattered pieces

I like to sit in the dark
I am content to sit in the dark
is anyone there?
Please let me be alone?
darkness, blackness, all around
it makes me go

contradicting gloom
I am afraid to end up alone
but I love to sit in the dark
and be content and lonely
A good cry, a good one
just to know I still can

go away
I am scared today
It'll pass
just leave me be
It'll pass

I am afraid to end up alone,
yet let me be lonely today.

CUT MY HEART

Beauty unseen
Show me love
Emotions untouched
surrounded, wanting
give me more
I'm exhausted
and very lonely
cut my heart
let it bleed
and at least I'll feel something
hurt me more
shout at the world
split me in two
shatter my hopes
let me be angry
it is better than feeling nonchalant
make me hate you
make me cry
because at least you tried
cut my heart
let it bleed
let it bleed
and make me feel something

SHUT IT OUT

something divine
and missing
shut it out
stop the noise
with this feeling
so discomforting
yet comfortable
a corner so mysterious
it blinds a judgement
look at me
you are not my release
but my insanity
heartless thoughts
piercing through you
stop. shut it out. redo.
scream in the dark
scream in the dark
SCREAM!
so divine and missing.
just shut it out.

A PAIN TOO DEEP

She looked slowly
as her heart broke from him
She looked sadly
as her life broke from the world
It took her in
It haunted her again
A pain too deep
no one wished it away
the little face
I couldn't take
when it would break
emotions so cold
it's not right
and it's not fair
but she was told that's life
A pain too deep
A pain too deep
that it wouldn't sleep
She looked slowly
as her heart broke from them

LITTLE PIECE

Beautiful and Changing
all the colors of the world
I see through you
yet I love you
just a little piece
just a little piece
No more a fool
needing and not wanting
just some little piece
I've found it here
and I see so clear
I see through you
and I love you too

WHEN TIME IS UP

the strangness wore off
and now it's just corrupt
it's like a bad run
like a blinding sun
what happened
I couldn't tell you
life is so funny
life is so funny
what will we do when we're
all done
it's like a bad run
like a blinding sun
what will we do?
what will we do?
when time is up

POLITICS

No fearless face nor man
a shadow that belongs to emptiness
is it regret? is it sin?
where are we going
why can't we begin?

someone once asked
where do you stand?
I don't stand
I don't know what is going on
how can I stand?
Stand on what view?

why are we here
why are we feeding others suffer?
Why are we there?
I don't know
I don't stand
I don't begin
Politics mean nothing

Printed in the United States
129223LV00015B/332/P

9 781432 717766